GAME CHANGER

ACCEPTING GOD'S ASSIGNMENT AND CHANGING THE STATUS QUO

RACHEL CARTER

Game Changer: Accepting God's Assignment and Changing the Status Quo

Copyright © 2022 Rachel Carter

Published by HigherLife Development Services, Inc.
PO Box 623307
Oviedo, Florida 32762
www.ahigherlife.com

ISBN: 978-1-958211-23-6 (Paperback)
ISBN: 978-1-958211-24-3 (ebook)
Library of Congress Control Number: 1-12087136349

Unless otherwise noted, all Scripture is taken from the New King James Version®. Copyright © 1982 by Thomas Nelson. Used by permission. All rights reserved.

Scripture quotations marked (KJV) are taken from the King James Version.

Scripture quotations marked (MSG) are taken from The Message. Copyright © by Eugene H. Peterson 1993, 1994, 1995, 1996, 2000, 2001, 2002. Used by permission of Tyndale House Publishers, Inc.

Scripture quotations marked (AMP) are taken from The Amplified® Bible, Copyright © 2015 by The Lockman Foundation. Used by permission. (www.Lockman.org.) All rights reserved.

Printed in the United States of America.

10 9 8 7 6 5 4 3 2 1

DEDICATION

This book is dedicated to my husband, Roderick V. Carter, whose unwavering love and support has given me liberty in the pursuit of Christ and His assignments for my life.

CONTENTS

FOREWORD

WE LIVE IN perilous times. Yet, in this season, God is raising up an elite band of "Special Forces" followers—believers who are willing to be equipped to understand the season and circumstances of the day and are prepared to be deployed by the Holy Spirit to change their surroundings.

The person who is called to such an important task must have a number of gifts and abilities. The chosen sons and daughters of the Father must have the capacity to swiftly operate many kinds of weapons, gadgets, vehicles, and equipment with precision, even under high-pressure conditions.

You are at war with spiritual giants, and the outcome of these levels of spiritual warfare have global consequences. There are threats of global pandemics, recession, and a third world war, just to mention a few.

The dimensions of spiritual warfare that the present-day Christian is engaged in is what is described in the Scriptures as battles with giants. When the children of Israel were journeying to the Promised Land, God spoke to them about giants. They were caught between their history and their destiny; and today, we are at that crossroads once again. But maintain your faith: The Promised Land is symbolic of the realm of the promises of God. It is a type and shadow of the manifestation of prophecy.

In the Scriptures, Moses sent twelve leaders into the Promised Land on an assignment to scope out the land. Upon their return, the overwhelming dread reported threw the whole nation of Israel into a state of fear and discouragement.

> *And they gave the children of Israel a bad report of the land which they had spied out, saying, "The land through which we have gone as spies is a land that devours its inhabitants, and all the people whom we saw in it are men of great stature. There we saw the giants (the descendants of Anak came from the giants); and we were like grasshoppers in our own sight, and so we were in their sight."*
>
> — Numbers 13:32-33

This was a mission-impossible-level assignment. It was a battle in the land of the giants. Ten out of the twelve spies came back with a report of evil. They were manipulated and intimidated by the size and strength of the giants. They lacked faith.

Just like then, the manifestation of your prophecy is in the land of giants. The promises of God always come to pass in the midst of impossibilities. Most of these leaders stated the facts and were moved by what they saw, but they did not walk by faith.

This is metaphorically what the magnitude and intensity of spiritual warfare is to the present-day Christian. It is a warfare with spiritual giants from city to city and from nation to nation.

The forces that determine history operate in two realms: The natural (physical) and the supernatural (spiritual). The events in the spiritual realm exercise a continuous and decisive influence on the events of the natural realm. The interplay of the events from these two realms defines the course of history.

The ramifications of the operations of these spiritual giants have socio-political, socio-financial, and geo-political consequences. This generation is dealing with massive global challenges that are pointing toward a crisis point, and that is why the stakes are so high.

Rachel Carter, a seasoned spiritual warrior and tremendously powerful woman of God, has written *Game Changer: Accepting God's Assignments and Changing the Status Quo* at such a strategic time as this. She operates under a unique and powerful apostolic and prophetic anointing which she uses through revelation and foresight to instruct, admonish, advocate, intercede, and edify the body of Christ.

I know that this adventure of the discovery of knowledge will equip you with the relevant faith and inner tenacity required to make you one of the finest agents for this global assignment.

You are on your way to becoming a global specialist, well-trained and prepared for the perilous times on the prophetic horizon of the nations. Live long, prosper, and fulfill your destiny in the mighty name of our Lord, Jesus Christ.

Bishop Senyo Bulla

INTRODUCTION

THE TIMES AND seasons demand for us to be girded and fortified with a greater level of faith, endurance, and strength. God is looking for those who are faithful, diligent, bold, and aggressive in their assignment as they pursue Him for the supernatural power of His grace to be manifested in and through them.

You have been selected, His sons, both men and women, who have reached a level of maturity and have been appointed to fulfill the assignments that God has revealed. Many will go through overwhelming odds to encounter His miraculous power and enforce His Kingdom agenda here on earth.

The Bible reveals that God wants you to know that He is orchestrating events to push you closer into birthing your destiny and has identified Himself as a woman in labor. It is His way of revealing that He is with you in all your trials, pain, and suffering, which is a catalyst to you giving birth to His plans and purposes.

I have held My peace a long time, I have been still and restrained Myself. Now I will cry like a woman in labor, I will pant and gasp at once.
— Isaiah 42:14

Isaiah encouraged and bought God's words of comfort to the people, saying:

Can a woman forget her nursing child, And not have compassion on the son of her womb? Surely they may forget, Yet I will not forget you.
— Isaiah 49:15

God will always take care of you. He will oversee your deliverance from all that you must endure and bring about your well-being. He cannot afford for you to not rise up and fulfill the divine strategies He has given you. You must continue to cry out to God and obtain His promises by faith. You will endure the birthing pains and have strength to give birth. The enemy will not be allowed to hinder you from fulfilling the plans and purposes of God.

I've learned to persevere and intercede relentlessly over the years concerning the successful completion of God's divine assignments for His sons and daughters. You are crucial to His plans, and He will make sure that you arrive at the designated place and position in Him and His Kingdom. God's Kingdom will not advance without you putting forth a level of hard work in intercession and spiritual warfare, which will always put you in a fortified and victorious position. It is a disservice to the Kingdom of God for you to refuse to act on or follow through on the prophetic directions that have been given to you. Thousands are waiting in each generation to benefit from what has been given to you in order to move His Kingdom to another phase. I challenge you to be diligent and patient with the process. I know what it is like.

After I accepted God's invitation of salvation, I found that I was functioning as an intercessor. I was like a fish out of water if I was not in the presence of God interceding as the Holy Spirit enables. It was in that realm that the prophetic anointing was birthed in me. I want to help as many people as possible by standing with them in intercession, that God would provide strategic guidance as you pursue His plan and purpose for your life.

Through good and troubling times, I had to put forth the effort to be consistent and not pull back or deviate from that assignment of intercession. I have written this book because I want you to know that you too can fulfill the call of God upon their lives, no matter the hindrances you may face. In this book, I share some of the revelation and training that the Spirit of God took me through over the years. It was such an awesome collaboration as He led, guided, corrected, and strengthened me. The years of training were of immeasurable value, and have given me confidence that in accepting new assignments, I am able to overcome and become victorious by faith in His divine abilities.

This book is a wake-up call with a deep concern for those who have become stagnant, discouraged, or lack the necessary revelation and skill to continue to pursue and fulfill their assignments. These sons must be dedicated to the cause and must be found in a state of readiness to advance the Kingdom of God.

God is looking for those who are willing to accept, by faith, the download of revelations to make sure that His nature and miraculous power are brought on the scene in the earthly realm. The evil circumstances that the enemy is using upon God's people must be broken. This is where you come in—you must increase the pressure upon the enemy until his hold on the sons of God is broken and the Kingdom agenda can advance.

You are a game changer, one who has been given the divine strategies to turn the tide around—to shift the hostile atmospheres into favorable conditions. God is counting on you to accept the assignment to unlock the heavens over individuals, families, communities, cities, and nations.

Will you be deeply committed and position yourself to become a burden bearer and to become successful in all that has been entrusted to you? With the unending help of God's grace, nothing shall be impossible to achieve!

Chapter 1

THE BURDEN BEARERS

*For the earnest expectation of the creature
waiteth for the manifestation of the sons of God.*
— Romans 8:19 KJV

GOD IS LOOKING for those who are willing and committed to enter into the realm of intercession. This is the vehicle, the method that He uses in order to bring His plan to reality—His sons who will preach His Gospel in each phase of the building of His Kingdom.

In a vision, God showed me His sons whom He had selected, anointed, and given the authority to advance His Kingdom. They were strategically positioned in communities throughout the world, equipping the Body of Christ. Many were using television, radio, social media, and internet. By the grace of God, these sons made great impact as they pushed forward the agenda of the Kingdom. They have tremendous influence that was felt throughout the nations and cities of this world. Their assignments—the burden that each was given—were slowly coming to an end.

As I stood in the vision, looking at these great men and women ministering, I saw them slowly falling backward and dropping the gilded scepters that they had held. I caught one of the scepters and stood in amazement at the intricate and gilded design, with one of the biggest sapphires I have ever seen at one end.

I asked the Lord what was happening, and He said that He was calling home His sons who had labored with Him, and their mantles were falling. Suddenly, I was overwhelmed by an agonizing pain and started to weep because I could not see anyone to pick up the scepters. I felt as though my heart was being pulled out of my chest.

> *I have millions of them that are waiting to come forth to preach My Gospel, just pray!*

The Lord said to me, "Pray for the release of My sons, who will preach My Gospel and bring about the divine alignment that is needed for the next phase of advancement for My Kingdom." I said, "But I don't see anyone!" He said, "I have millions of them that are waiting to come forth to preach My Gospel, just pray!"

Over the years, the Holy Spirit led me into intercession at 2:00 a.m. every morning as He used my intercession to aggressively demand the manifestation of the sons of

God. This burden came with urgency and much grace as I embarked on this assignment. I was given instructions concerning the different areas and countries for which to strategically target my prayers.

I ran to get into the presence of the Lord, to labor with Him, never changing the prayer focus until I was given new instructions. There were times that I prayed the same prayers for months, sometimes years, before receiving new instructions. I was selected to become a burden bearer!

Some of you have been travailing and waiting patiently for the manifestation of the plans of God. A summons has been issued for your fire to be placed on the altars! Your prayers are deeply coveted by God, and the Holy Spirit is in great anticipation to move and allow His power to show up.

You are engaged in combat with spiritual giants, and the outcome of these contentions have global consequences.

In every generation and phase of the advancement of God's Kingdom, you will find countless burden bearers who have successfully fulfilled their purposes and the Lord has now called them to be with Him. Others are in the midst of their assignments, and many more are strategically positioning themselves to receive and accept the prayer burden.

I command you to posture yourselves in the birthing position to give birth to the mind of God!

Chapter 2

THE BURDEN OF INTERCESSION

A PRAYER BURDEN IS a deep spiritual concern in the heart and mind of God that is revealed by the Holy Spirit to those who have been given a gift for intercession.

Nehemiah, in his role as a governor and as a leader in rebuilding the walls of Jerusalem, is an example of the importance of intercession. His spiritual depth is revealed as a man of prayer and influence by the fact that he inspired the people to rise up and rebuild the broken-down walls in only fifty-two days, despite intense opposition from inside and outside the city.

In order for Nehemiah to be successful in his assignment, he had to go through these three stages.

1. **The burden of intercession.** This is where God has chosen the method by which He will impart the burden.

*The words of Nehemiah the son of Hachaliah.
It came to pass in the month of Chislev, in the
twentieth year, as I was in Shushan the citadel, that Hanani one of my brethren came
with men from Judah; and I asked them concerning the Jews who had escaped, who had
survived the captivity, and concerning Jerusalem. And they said to me, "The survivors
who are left from the captivity in the province
are there in great distress and reproach. The
wall of Jerusalem is also broken down, and its
gates are burned with fire." So it was, when I
heard these words, that I sat down and wept,
and mourned for many days; I was fasting and
praying before the God of heaven.*

—Nehemiah 1:1-4

2. **The content of his intercession.** Nehemiah
described in detail the purpose for which he cried
out to God for help. He left no stone unturned as
he positioned himself in fasting and prayer, with
great humility and reverence toward God's character, nature, ways, and Word.

*And I said: "I pray, LORD God of heaven, O
great and awesome God, You who keep Your
covenant and mercy with those who love You
and observe Your commandments, please let
Your ear be attentive and Your eyes open,*

that You may hear the prayer of Your servant which I pray before You now, day and night, for the children of Israel Your servants, and confess the sins of the children of Israel which we have sinned against You. Both my father's house and I have sinned. We have acted very corruptly against You, and have not kept the commandments, the statutes, nor the ordinances which You commanded Your servant Moses. Remember, I pray, the word that You commanded Your servant Moses, saying, 'If you are unfaithful, I will scatter you among the nations; but if you return to Me, and keep My commandments and do them, though some of you were cast out to the farthest part of the heavens, yet I will gather them from there, and bring them to the place which I have chosen as a dwelling for My name.' Now these are Your servants and Your people, whom You have redeemed by Your great power, and by Your strong hand. O Lord, I pray, please let Your ear be attentive to the prayer of Your servant, and to the prayer of Your servants who desire to fear Your name; and let Your servant prosper this day, I pray, and grant him mercy in the sight of this man." For I was the king's cupbearer.

—Nehemiah 1:5-11

3. **The outcome of his intercession with King Artaxerxes.** God moved upon the heart and mind of the king so that Nehemiah was granted favor. The king made him the governor of Jerusalem and provided him letters to get all the supplies he would need from the different territories in order to fulfill the assignment of rebuilding the walls.

> *And it came to pass in the month of Nisan, in the twentieth year of King Artaxerxes, when wine was before him, that I took the wine and gave it to the king. Now I had never been sad in his presence before. Therefore the king said to me, "Why is your face sad, since you are not sick? This is nothing but sorrow of heart." So I became dreadfully afraid, and said to the king, "May the king live forever! Why should my face not be sad, when the city, the place of my fathers' tombs, lies waste, and its gates are burned with fire?" Then the king said to me, "What do you request?" So I prayed to the God of heaven. And I said to the king, "If it pleases the king, and if your servant has found favor in your sight, I ask that you send me to Judah, to the city of my fathers' tombs, that I may rebuild it." Then the king said to me (the queen also sitting beside him), "How long will your journey be? And when will you return?"*

So it pleased the king to send me; and I set him a time. Furthermore I said to the king, "If it pleases the king, let letters be given to me for the governors of the region beyond the River, that they must permit me to pass through till I come to Judah, and a letter to Asaph the keeper of the king's forest, that he must give me timber to make beams for the gates of the citadel which pertains to the temple, for the city wall, and for the house that I will occupy." And the king granted them to me according to the good hand of my God upon me.

—Nehemiah 2:1-8

Can we navigate skillfully like Nehemiah and be successful in our assignments? The Bible records that he went before God in prayer or intercession at least eleven times. He had to be a man who was frequently in the presence of God. He travailed in prayer as the assignment took over his spirit. His prayers were very short, but they came forth from his heart and zeal for the things of God.

He was one of the main examples of a praying leader who accomplished impossible tasks because of his dependence on God.

Chapter 3

FOR THIS CAUSE

THERE MUST BE an assignment given in order for one to have a cause. It takes deep commitment to an outcome or movement for one to have the ability to rise up in action to defend and advocate for it.

David had a cause to defend the name of God and bring about the downfall of Goliath so that Israel could be victorious in the war against the Philistines. He was sent by his father to bring provisions and to check up on his brothers who were in the army to fight against the Philistines. They were paralyzed by fear; Goliath's stature and skills had intimidated King Saul and his army. But David trusted in God and said that he could kill Goliath. David's brothers demanded for him to be quiet and to go back home, but David saw an opportunity to bring God's power on the scene and destroy the enemy.

> *And David said, "What have I done now? Is there not a cause?"*
>
> — 1 Samuel 17:29

David's confidence in God and His abilities, his aggressiveness and boldness, were seen by his brothers as arrogance and over-confidence in his own abilities. Many in
the Body of Christ believe that they have the right to put
down, berate, and speak against those who are pursuing
God with the aggressiveness of great faith.

> *Then David said to the Philistine, "You come to
> me with a sword, with a spear, and with a jav-
> elin. But I come to you in the name of the LORD
> of hosts, the God of the armies of Israel, whom
> you have defied. This day the LORD will deliver
> you into my hand, and I will strike you and
> take your head from you. And this day I will
> give the carcasses of the camp of the Philistines
> to the birds of the air and the wild beasts of the
> earth, that all the earth may know that there
> is a God in Israel. Then all this assembly shall
> know that the LORD does not save with sword
> and spear; for the battle is the LORD's, and He
> will give you into our hands." So it was, when
> the Philistine arose and came and drew near to
> meet David, that David hurried and ran toward
> the army to meet the Philistine. Then David put
> his hand in his bag and took out a stone; and he
> slung it and struck the Philistine in his forehead,*

*so that the stone sank into his forehead, and he
fell on his face to the earth.*

— 1 Samuel 17:45-49

David answered the call to be commissioned by God to
defend His honor and deal with the threats of the enemy.
What Saul and his army could not accomplish, David did,
through faith in God.

God is always looking for someone who will accept an
assignment. Will you?

*Also I heard the voice of the Lord, saying:
"Whom shall I send, And who will go for Us?"
Then I said, "Here am I! Send me."*

— Isaiah 6:8

Isaiah the prophet answered the call of God, but saw
himself as being unworthy of the assignment. God had
to take away the condemna-
tion of sin and assured him
that He, Jehovah, had qualified and approved his ministry. Isaiah's willingness to
be commissioned was evi-
dent, for he served God the rest of his life.

> *God is always looking
> for someone who will
> accept an assignment.
> Will you?*

Let us take a look at how King Hezekiah was victorious
in battle as he prepared and stirred up his people's confidence in God.

King Hezekiah saw that Sennacherib, king of Assyria, came to fight against Jerusalem, so he strengthened himself and gave instructions to the people about how to prepare. He inspired faith and strength, reminding them that God would help them and fight their battle. The Bible records that the people rested on the words of Hezekiah. They trusted in their leader's great faith in God's abilities, his boldness and courageous actions that brought about the results which showed that God was with him.

> *Then they called out with a loud voice in Hebrew to the people of Jerusalem who were on the wall, to frighten them and trouble them, that they might take the city. And they spoke against the God of Jerusalem, as against the gods of the people of the earth—the work of men's hands. Now because of this King Hezekiah and the prophet Isaiah, the son of Amoz, prayed and cried out to heaven. Then the LORD sent an angel who cut down every mighty man of valor, leader, and captain in the camp of the king of Assyria. So he returned shamefaced to his own land. And when he had gone into the temple of his god, some of his own offspring struck him down with the sword there. Thus the LORD saved Hezekiah and the inhabitants of Jerusalem from the hand of Sennacherib the*

king of Assyria, and from the hand of all others,
and guided them on every side.
— 2 Chronicles 32:18-22

Our leaders must be strong men and women of great faith who stir their people to rise up with the necessary actions to stop the enemy's advancement and give him a crushing blow. Their assignment is directly related to the purposes for which God has preordained them. They can either discover the assignment and rise up with the corresponding actions of great faith in God, or choose to be paralyzed by fear, the opinions of man, and allow their destinies and congregations to be derailed so that they will never fulfill their purposes—God's plan for their life.

How tragic that so many are under the crippling spirit of fear and have accepted adverse conditions as normal! To those leaders who are not protecting and building up the faith of the people—beware! God is faithfully watching over His Kingdom.

These end-times leaders must not allow the enemy to derail them from their assignments. They must maintain their anointing, their authority, and must not compromise!

Chapter 4

LOSS OF AUTHORITY

MANY WHO WERE commissioned by God started out upholding His standards with passion and zeal, but over time, the enemy used very subtle devices to lure and seduce them to preach a gospel that did not represent the true nature of God.

These individuals have a charismatic character that is girded with an underlying desire for power and have not presented Christ consistently. Instead, they have drawn the people to themselves. This creates instability in the Body.

The people have not learned about God and His ways. The messages preached make people feel good, catching them up in a state of euphoria. Scriptures are quoted, but only for a quick fix, not to point the way to Christ. The people pursue a personality and do not receive the joy of the Lord.

This is a plot of the enemy to spread the poison of a spirit of error through those who have the ability to influence the Body and the masses who follow them. This poison is released in very small doses over time so that many are deceived. Their spirits become dull; they lose the ability to hear the voice of God. Lethargy sets in.

> *For the time will come when they will not endure sound doctrine, but according to their own desires, because they have itching ears, they will heap up for themselves teachers; and they will turn their ears away from the truth, and be turned aside to fables.*
>
> — 2 Timothy 4:3-4

Those preaching these messages pull away from those who will provide good counsel, give spiritual oversight, and encourage remaining true to Christ. What an evil plot of the enemy—using man's innate desire for power and notoriety that is embedded in their pride. Such deception!

In an article titled, "Oil spill reveals the dangers of success," Robert J. Samuelson stated that "success tends to breed carelessness and complacency" and that "it is human nature to celebrate success by relaxing." He further stated that "the challenge we face is how to acknowledge this urge without being duped by it."[1]

One must closely watch over the seasons of success and great achievements. You must refuse to allow the twin

---

1   Robert J. Samuelson. "Oil spill reveals the dangers of success," *Daily Herald*, accessed August 19, 2022, https://www.heraldextra. com/news/2010/jun/08/oil-spill-reveals-the-dangers-of-success/.

companions, carelessness and complacency, to enter into your season of harvest. Do not be fooled by the level of elevation and believe that nothing can stop, slow down, or derail you at this level. Your ignorance of the strategies of the devil or the innate desires of unconverted, unregenerate human agents will be used to take you down, and as they say, "You will come to a screeching halt."

> *His watchmen are blind, They are all ignorant;*
> *They are all dumb dogs, They cannot bark;*
> *Sleeping, lying down, loving to slumber.*
> — Isaiah 56:10

This applies to the leaders who have been given the responsibility to take extreme care in looking after the souls of men, to feed them with knowledge and understanding, but are not qualified for the job. They are blind and ignorant of things that are divine and spiritual. They are spiritually dead and are useless. They do not reprove the errors and vices of men or warn them of their danger. Jesus called such leaders blind guides, and blind leaders of the blind! He was directing the disciples' attention to leaders who held responsibility, but were not fit for the

> *You must refuse to allow the twin companions, carelessness and complacency, to enter into your season of harvest.*

role. Jesus was teaching about the motives of men in ascending to positions of influence and carrying vain titles by exposing their character.

> *Let them alone. They are blind leaders of the blind. And if the blind leads the blind, both will fall into a ditch.*
>
> — Matthew 15:14

We need leaders who are yielded and willing to serve God and His purposes. They need to have spiritual sight and to be capable of alerting people of danger, discovering and identifying the enemies within and outside the church, assessing the level of the impending dangers, and swiftly countering the strategies of the enemy against the people and Church of the Living God. Where are those who can walk in that level of authority?

> *Thus says the LORD of hosts: "If you will walk in My ways, And if you will keep My command, Then you shall also judge My house, And likewise have charge of My courts; I will give you places to walk Among these who stand here."*
>
> — Zechariah 3:7

Chapter 5

THE CHURCH MUST GOVERN

NATIONS AND CULTURES are in a constant state of change. Many are attempting to leverage themselves to become power brokers in the affairs of this world. Some are rising, others are falling, and treaties are being forged among them for good as well as for evil. Many of them are experiencing much unrest and instability.

The shaking of the economic and political systems of the nations of the world is like a volcano that has been experiencing small eruptions for years. We have become accustomed to it and it gives no fear to those hearing and feeling its rumblings. Suddenly, a massive eruption ensues, and many are dazed by its sheer volatility.

Some have prophesied of this as a vehicle that God will use to bring the kingdoms of this world under His authority. The travailing of the earth through monumental disasters is increasing while the earth's population is exploding and people are building on belief systems that are deceptive and unstable. They will come to the Body to find solutions to their problems.

God is preparing His Church to be the answer to man's challenges, and He has to equip it to govern the affairs of this world. The political and economic systems of this world are in step with the preparation that is taking place in the Body.

But with every crisis that humanity faces, special people are chosen to help lead the way back to the Promised Land—to remind us all of what God has promised in His infinite wisdom.

God is the one orchestrating everything. He is allowing adverse circumstances to create the right amount of pressure that will cause His children to conform to His ways, exposing the areas that man has failed to trust God in. He must maintain the integrity of His Name. He is immutable.

Allow the Hand of God to propel you throughout the seasons to be found in the right place, in the right time, with the right people.

We must build our lives on the Kingdom of God in order for us not to be shaken by what is taking place in the world systems. We must neither fear it nor be derailed by it.

There is much unrest and instability in the economic and political systems of our nations, but we must be found walking in the divine blessings of God. Allow the Hand of God to propel you throughout the seasons to be found in the right place, in the right time, with the right people.

> *And Jesus answered and said to them: "Take heed that no one deceives you. For many will come in My name, saying, 'I am the Christ,' and will deceive many. And you will hear of wars and rumors of wars. See that you are not troubled; for all these things must come to pass, but the end is not yet."*
>
> — Matthew 24:4-6

The Body must rise to the level of faith in God and put His divine strategies into operation. It is time for the Church of the Living God to rise up and pray!

Chapter 6

THE PREVAILING ANOINTING: PRAYER AND FASTING

Then it came to pass the seventh time, that he said, "There is a cloud, as small as a man's hand, rising out of the sea!" So he said, "Go up, say to Ahab, 'Prepare your chariot, and go down before the rain stops you.'" Now it happened in the meantime that the sky became black with clouds and wind, and there was a heavy rain. So Ahab rode away and went to Jezreel. Then the hand of the LORD came upon Elijah; and he girded up his loins and ran ahead of Ahab to the entrance of Jezreel.

— 1 Kings 18:44-46

THROUGH THE ORCHESTRATION of God's divine Hand, we find Elijah at the top of Mt. Carmel after an epic contest. His weapons were prayer, fasting, and faith. He had confronted and killed the prophets of Baal. Elijah had to travail in order to give birth to this prevailing anointing.

You must spend time there in the presence of God, wanting Him and desiring for His will be done in and through you, digging into His Word, being aware of His greatness and power, waiting to feel His presence, and knowing that without Him you cannot do anything but with Him nothing is impossible.

You must sacrifice your time and resources and position yourself in the presence of God and earnestly desire more of Him. As you contend for this anointing, the Holy Spirit will open the heavens and rain down the supernatural power of God in and through you. You will be thoroughly equipped and furnished with everything that you need for your assignment.

You must be diligent in deploying the weapons of fasting and prayer!

This anointing, birthed out of fasting and prayer, will give you an injection of faith in God. He will give you a thrust that shifts you into a place of destiny, a place where you can prosper and walk into the blessings of God. It is in that position of being in the presence of God that you will shift rapidly past all opposition and overtake all that God has promised. We need to contend in this season for this type of anointing.

Esther fasted and prayed in order for the Jews to be saved from annihilation. The Bible records that she employed the weapon of fasting in order for God to use her as she intervened for the Jews.

Then Esther told them to reply to Mordecai: "Go, gather all the Jews who are present in Shushan, and fast for me; neither eat nor drink for three days, night or day. My maids and I will fast likewise. And so I will go to the king, which is against the law; and if I perish, I perish!" So Mordecai went his way and did according to all that Esther commanded him.

— Esther 4:15-17

Now it happened on the third day that Esther put on her royal robes and stood in the inner court of the king's palace, across from the king's house, while the king sat on his royal throne in the royal house, facing the entrance of the house. So it was, when the king saw Queen Esther standing in the court, that she found favor in his sight, and the king held out to Esther the golden scepter that was in his hand. Then Esther went near and touched the top of the scepter. And the king said to her, "What do you wish, Queen

Esther? What is your request? It shall be given to you—up to half the kingdom!"

— Esther 5:1-3

You will never have access to the spiritual realm of power without the enabling power of the Holy Spirit. He is anticipating your hunger and zeal for notable evidence of God's supremacy. You must be diligent in deploying the weapons of fasting and prayer! It must be part of your lifestyle!

WEAPONIZE

THE HOLY GHOST is responsible for weaponizing us, and we will never experience success and have tremendous breakthroughs without His enabling power.

According to Webster's Dictionary, the word *weaponize* means "to adapt for use as a weapon of war."

The Holy Ghost—the dispenser of the "Supernova" of all power and authority in heaven and earth—is the one that brings in the tangible providence of God in and through His children. The sons are given a level of supernatural ability to govern in this realm in Christ. In order to operate in this dimension, we must take care to forge a vital, passionate, and intimate relationship with Him.

We must pursue God for the strategies and strength that is needed for the manifestation of the sons of God.

He needs man to enter into the realm of intercession. This is the vehicle, the method that He uses in order to bring His plan into action—His sons who will preach His Gospel in each phase of the building of His Kingdom.

We need the power of the Holy Ghost to endure the different stages of the processes that God has designed just for us, to help us to embrace what does not feel or taste good. For each process there is a guarantee of the increase of the Kingdom in us.

God was able to use Gideon in the Book of Judges who was full of fear and hiding from the enemy to thresh wheat. He took a stand against his father and countrymen and trusted in God's divine abilities. God strengthened and instilled boldness and courage within him. Gideon went from weak faith to a man of great faith and was victorious in destroying and driving away the enemy because of his willingness to obey God and availability to be used by God.

God cannot be outmaneuvered in battle.

God cannot be outmaneuvered in battle. His people will always have the advantage and triumph in any terrain.

God gives ability to men, but you cannot make an able man faithful. That is why God looks out for those who are faithful—willing and available so He can make them able. He gives ability to those He has chosen!

The gifts and skills are given to you for the success of your ministry and manifestations of the power of God in and through you. He will use challenges to force you to upgrade your weapons, which must always be sharpened and ready.

We find in the Scriptures that God sent a prophet to instruct the king of Israel to fortify himself and the nation because the king of Syria would declare war on Israel. They had a year in which to put in place all that was needed for the upcoming battle.

> *And the prophet came to the king of Israel and said to him, "Go, strengthen yourself; take note, and see what you should do, for in the spring of the year the king of Syria will come up against you."*
>
> — 1 Kings 20:22

God will identify the enemy and give divine instructions for tremendous victories. The ability to follow His instructions is directly related to the level of success you will have. You will be armed with enough pertinent information. He is depending on you!

God's power is the force behind the use of your weapons.

> *And Moses said to the children of Israel, "See, the LORD has called by name Bezalel the son of Uri, the son of Hur, of the tribe of Judah; and He has filled him with the Spirit of God, in wisdom and understanding, in knowledge and all manner of workmanship, to design artistic works, to work in gold and silver and bronze, in cutting jewels for setting, in carving wood, and*

to work in all manner of artistic workmanship. And He has put in his heart the ability to teach, in him and Aholiab the son of Ahisamach, of the tribe of Dan. He has filled them with skill to do all manner of work of the engraver and the designer and the tapestry maker, in blue, purple, and scarlet thread, and fine linen, and of the weaver—those who do every work and those who design artistic works."

— Exodus 35:30-35

The Spirit of God must release a dimension of God's grace upon you so that you can move the Kingdom agenda forward.

But this is what was spoken by the prophet Joel: "And it shall come to pass in the last days, says God, That I will pour out of My Spirit on all flesh; Your sons and your daughters shall prophesy, Your young men shall see visions, Your old men shall dream dreams. And on My menservants and on My maidservants I will pour out My Spirit in those days; And they shall prophesy. I will show wonders in heaven above And signs in the earth beneath: Blood and fire and vapor of smoke."

— Acts 2:16-19

You must be sharpened by the Word of God and skillful in its use.

> *For the word of God is living and powerful, and sharper than any two-edged sword, piercing even to the division of soul and spirit, and of joints and marrow, and is a discerner of the thoughts and intents of the heart.*
>
> — Hebrews 4:12

> *The sword of the Spirit, which is the word of God.*
>
> — Ephesians 6:17b

The Word of God enables us to be effective in our calling. You must be dedicated, committed, and able to execute relevant actions to stay true to your cause.

> *The secret things belong to the LORD our God, but those things which are revealed belong to us and to our children forever, that we may do all the words of this law.*
>
> — Deuteronomy 29:29

God's plan for mankind cannot be hijacked or derailed. He is patient and is not insecure about man's inability. His grace is more than sufficient as He works out His divine purposes. God will not allow the enemy to come up against you without providing battle strategies. You will win every battle by the grace of God!

Chapter 8

PREVAILING IN TURBULENT TIMES

I WAS ON A plane traveling, and about forty minutes before landing we were informed by the pilot that there was turbulence ahead. The pilot prepared us by giving the instructions to return to our seats and fasten our seat belts. Suddenly, the plane stated to shake, the white clouds gave way to dark clouds, and we continued to ascend to a higher altitude. A few times it seemed as though the plane dropped a few hundred feet before rising back to its designated altitude. Finally, we were above the atmospheric climate that was responsible for the turbulence.

God's people must be found prevailing in turbulent times. He has given you the power and ability to function at a particular level of authority so that you can rise up above anything that would attempt to destabilize, confront, or possibly take you out. The level of authority you operate in will determine your ability to out-strategize the enemy and be at a place of advantage.

You will not fulfill the plans of God if you do not become a warrior and engage in spiritual warfare! This is a key to fulfilling your calling. We are in a spiritual battle and it will take consistent hard work in the different phases of combat you will encounter to subdue the enemy and prevail in all different terrains and atmospheric climates.

Prayer is hard labor and requires a lot of effort. Your intercession is like a covert operation that needs stealth, precision, patience, wisdom, consistency, power, adaptability, and the ability to walk in a consecrated, strong, vibrant, passionate, and intense relationship with the Holy Spirit.

God is looking for the intercessors to rise up and labor consistently in a certain level of spiritual warfare so that they can be given divine strategies to help usher in the manifestation of His divine purposes in and through His sons for His redemptive plan.

These individuals are a threat to the enemy's diabolical plans and will encounter intense opposition. The enemy has always targeted those who have accepted their God-given assignments and are faithful! God's plan will come to pass, and He needs you to succeed regardless of the attacks and opposition that will come against the precious cargo that you carry.

Since God has so generously let us in on what he is doing, we're not about to throw up our hands and walk off the job just because we run into occasional hard times. We refuse to wear masks and play games. We don't maneuver and manipulate behind the scenes. And we don't twist God's Word to suit ourselves. Rather, we keep everything we do and say out in the open, the whole truth on display, so that those who want to can see and judge for themselves in the presence of God.

— 2 Corinthians 4:1-2 MSG

Do not allow people to download an overload of their failures and fear upon you. It will weigh you down and cause you to stay idle on the runways that were meant for you to take off and triumph.

In Exodus 13 and 14, Moses sent twelve spies to check out the land that God had promised them. Ten brought back fearful reports—they said the people there were giants, and their cities were large and fortified. Their report frightened the Israelites, and they cried

> *Do not allow people to download an overload of their failures and fear upon you.*

out to Moses in fear. Two spies—Joshua and Caleb—brought back a report that God was with the nation of Israel, that they should not be afraid because they would devour the enemies and possess the land that God promised them. Millions did not have confidence in God's abilities, even though they had seen the miracles He performed for their deliverance from Egypt. They died in the wilderness and never made it to the territories that God had for them to settle and live prosperous lives. Only Caleb and Joshua were allowed to receive God's promises, because they came back with amazing faith to subdue the enemy and possess the land which God had given. Are you able to believe God and push past all opposition? Can you stand with God when others will not?

God will download His divine revelation so you can walk in authority and take control of the environment that He has sent you into. You must walk in power and authority to control a spiritual climate. The battle will be won by those who control the spiritual climate. When you operate in a level of spiritual power, you will subdue all opposition and contention, have financial control, and determine the type of season you will have.

Chapter 9

STAY IN YOUR LANE

RECENTLY PURCHASED A car and accidentally activated the "stay in your lane assist mode." If you veer outside the markings of the lane that you are driving in, whether to the right or left, the computer in the car takes control of the steering wheel and will steer the car back into your lane. The control was taken out of my hands for a few seconds even though I had a firm grip on the steering wheel. That was very alarming! This happened at least twice within two days, and each time it shook me up for a few minutes as I tried to figure out why my car was responding the way it did. I was informed by a ser-

> *Ignorance is an enemy that undermines your ability to stay on course and be successful.*

vice representative that there was nothing wrong with my car and that I had activated the "stay in your lane assist mode," a safety feature located on the steering wheel. I had to confirm with them that a green light with a car between two lines was now showing up on my console.

Ignorance is an enemy that undermines your ability to stay on course and be successful.

Look at how many times I veered off track as I was driving, and if I did not have the technology for the computer to take control, I could have ended up in an accident, possibly with a tragic outcome. This is one way the enemy brings opposition which causes us to veer off course and be derailed. How many are not able to hear the voice of the Holy Spirit alerting them to be cautious and shift in one direction or the other to stay on track? How many are stubborn to their detriment in the direction that they believe is the right one because they could not hear or position themselves to hear the voice of God?

Lack of knowledge makes us ineffective or unfruitful.

God opened my eyes to a few enemies that can derail or bring delays in your assignments. Here are two that are destiny killers—*ignorance and the inability to hear the voice of God in order to stay on track.*

Ignorance must never be allowed to embed itself as your companion.

One's level of interpretation or understanding of something is directly related to the level of effectiveness in the use of that matter. Lack of knowledge makes us ineffective or unfruitful in the use of a thing. Just as the flow of communication is essential for effectiveness or fruitfulness, so is understanding of a structure and the processes that have been established in any system. This is essential for progress and success.

The failure to gain the necessary knowledge or information for the correct use of some thing or system is a setup for setbacks, delay, and non-accomplishment. So it is when we fail to put forth the effort to know God, His ways, and apply that knowledge to our lives. Our lack of understanding of His Kingdom and its operation hinders us from being effective or fruitful.

This requires much meekness and humility.

He needs us, His children, to have a level of intimacy with Him in order to receive His divine revelation so we can fulfill our assignments. You must be consistent in demonstrating His supernatural divine nature to manifest the measure of His power and authority in every phase of the building up of His Kingdom.

Getting the right interpretation is crucial to be able to see and place the worth or value of His purposes in the right position in your heart, mind, and soul so that you can willingly serve Him and His purposes.

Whether or not you understand or agree does not change the fact that God is who He is, in His love, nature, and character.

- He does not need your opinion or advice.

- He will not violate or break His rules just because you feel you deserve something.

- He is in total control of everything in heaven and earth.

- He expects us to prosper in everything, in thought, word, and deed.

- He uses evil and good to equip and empower us—to prosper us.

- He opens up our eyes to His position or thoughts concerning the challenges that confront us day after day.

- He is a good Father.

- He loves us and demonstrated it before we knew about Him.

- God has done everything to ensure that we prosper.

It is up to us to gain understanding of Him, His Kingdom, and its rules so that we can put a halt to all that is contrary to His will. What is true or false is independent of what we think is true or false. Our perception does not change facts. Our level of understanding or interpretation of something does not change it.

The ability to focus, hear the voice of God, and stay on track is vital to the success of your assignment.

One must be cognizant that in the season where destinies are manifesting, they must draw closer to God for direction and cannot afford to lose focus. They must be able to hear clearly from God for the necessary instructions.

You have an advantage. God is on your side, and He will work in and through all things to ensure that you prosper! You need divine revelation in order to focus and stay true to the assignment given you, so you can walk in authority.

Elijah had just confronted the prophets of Baal and dealt with the witchcraft of the treacherous Jezebel and now ran away into a place of despair at Horeb. He needed to hear the voice of God in order to get the new instructions that can pull him out of despair and discouragement. He needed a fresh revelation—divine impartation—so that there could be a change in his pessimistic idea that he was alone in the assignment and there was no one else available to help God.

Never believe that you are the only one uniquely qualified to help God.

Never believe that you are the only one uniquely qualified to help God. He will always commission others to fulfill the overall objective for His mandate. Never get to the point where you start responding like you are the only one who is true and available.

Many have fallen prey to the erroneous mindset of believing that you have given your all and now have nothing left to continue in the assignment. This is where many stumble into pits of discouragement from battle weariness. Many will experience this syndrome that is brought on by the repercussions of intense warfare that they have been engaged in.

Elijah needed fresh revelation or instructions in order to move forward. God strategically led him to a place where he could rest, regain his focus, hear from God, and obey.

> *And there he went into a cave, and spent the night in that place; and behold, the word of the LORD came to him, and He said to him, "What are you doing here, Elijah?" So he said, "I have been very zealous for the LORD God of hosts; for the children of Israel have forsaken Your covenant, torn down Your altars, and killed Your prophets with the sword. I alone am left; and they seek to take my life." Then He said, "Go out, and stand on the mountain before the LORD." And behold, the LORD passed by, and a great and strong wind tore into the mountains and broke the rocks in pieces before the LORD, but the LORD was not in the wind; and after the wind an earthquake, but the LORD was not in the earthquake; and after the earthquake a fire, but the LORD was not in the fire; and after the fire a still small voice. So it was, when Elijah heard it, that he wrapped his face in his mantle and went out and stood in the entrance of the cave. Suddenly a voice came to him, and*

*said, "What are you doing here, Elijah?" And
he said, "I have been very zealous for the LORD
God of hosts; because the children of Israel have
forsaken Your covenant, torn down Your altars,
and killed Your prophets with the sword. I alone
am left; and they seek to take my life." Then the
LORD said to him: "Go, return on your way
to the Wilderness of Damascus; and when you
arrive, anoint Hazael as king over Syria. Also
you shall anoint Jehu the son of Nimshi as king
over Israel. And Elisha the son of Shaphat of
Abel Meholah you shall anoint as prophet in
your place. It shall be that whoever escapes the
sword of Hazael, Jehu will kill; and whoever
escapes the sword of Jehu, Elisha will kill. Yet
I have reserved seven thousand in Israel, all
whose knees have not bowed to Baal, and every
mouth that has not kissed him."*

— 1 Kings 19:9-18

In the vision in which I saw scepters falling and no one
picking them up, I cried out in desperation and felt as
though the burden of intercession was too much. How
can I intercede for so many for their destinies to be fulfilled? God said to me, "They are there, just pray!" I said,
"I don't see anyone." He responded by saying, "I have millions of them that are waiting to come forth to preach My
Gospel, just pray!"

Do you have the capacity, the intimacy in your relationship with the Holy Spirit, to hear the voice of God when He changes the manner in which He chooses to communicate as well as the direction you need to go? Be determined to position yourself to hear His voice and blot out all distractions in order to follow His instructions. Have you developed your gifts and employed all the principles that God has imparted to you over the course of time so that you have developed a vital, passionate relationship with Him? The mature ones, the sons of God, must rise up and fulfill their assignments!

> *Be determined to bulldoze everything that will hinder your relationship with God and His plans.*

Let God take over and get you back on track! He will never allow you to go on this journey without taking you through a time of preparation. Be sensitive to His voice and be determined to bulldoze everything that will hinder your relationship with God and His plans. You must continue to identify the forces that have been unleashed against you and those who are around you.

Chapter 10

COMBINE FORCES

OD'S WILL FOR us is to not go beyond what He has revealed to us through His Word by our actions and thoughts. We are not to wander away from His Word nor wander to the left or to the right. When one makes a decision to move forward on something and does not apply due diligence to the matter to ensure that the information is accurate, then that one has fallen into the trap of "presumption." The enemy uses the combined forces of criticism and pride to stop you and those who are part of your assignment from moving forward. Together they give birth to presumption, which can impede one's spiritual development and understanding. It will hinder you from obtaining the fresh revelation of God and walking in total victory.

I must expose these two forces that always conspire to trip us up! You need the knowledge of their characteristics and operations so you can identify them and execute God's divine strategies to find deliverance from their strong ill intent and hidden agendas.

Pride

Synonyms for pride in the Bible are "insolence," "presumptuousness," "arrogance," "conceit," "high-mindedness," and "haughtiness," and "egotism."

Charles Spurgeon, in his sermon "On Humbling Ourselves Before God," described pride as "an all-pervading sin." He said,

> *Pride is so natural to fallen man that it springs up in his heart like weeds in a well-watered garden … its every touch is evil. You may hunt down this fox, and think you have destroyed it, and lo! Your very exultation is pride. None have more pride than those who dream that they have none. Pride is a sin with a thousand lives; it seems impossible to kill it.*[2]

> **Most people are unaware of their pride, and that is where the danger lies.**

Most people are unaware of their pride, and that is where the danger lies.

---

2   Charles Spurgeon, "On Humbling Ourselves Before God," The Spurgeon Center, accessed August 24, 2022, https://www.spurgeon.org/resource-library/sermons/on-humbling-ourselves-before-god/#flipbook/.

Pride goes before destruction, And a haughty spirit before a fall.

— Proverbs 16:18

The Bible records that pride was the enemy that caused the downfall of many! It was the sin of pride that led to the oppression of the people of Israel and Judah (Isa. 3). James 4:6 tells us that God opposes the proud but gives grace to the humble. Many are not able to prosper and fulfill their destinies because of pride.

For men will be lovers of themselves, lovers of money, boasters, proud, blasphemers, disobedient to parents, unthankful, unholy, unloving, unforgiving, slanderers, without self-control, brutal, despisers of good, traitors, headstrong, haughty, lovers of pleasure rather than lovers of God.

— 2 Timothy 3:2-4

Pride causes you to change direction and focus on yourself. Everything is now about seeking personal attention and coveting the praises of others, not about pointing the praises of others toward God. It causes us to be selfish and loveless. Our decisions will always be for personal gain.

Criticism

The definition of criticism is:

- the expression of disapproval of someone or something based on perceived faults or mistakes.

- the act of judging unfavorably or faultfinding.

There is a major difference between helping someone develop and improve and having a critical spirit. A critical spirit is never satisfied, and it always expects and finds disappointment. This sin will always tear down the one who is dishing it out and the one that it is being heaped upon. No good will come out of this act.

> *A critical spirit is never satisfied, and it always expects and finds disappointment.*

Godly criticism is grounded in love and comes from one who is humble and pure. Our intent should never be malicious. Paul said in Ephesians 4:29, "Let no corrupt word proceed out of your mouth, but what is good for necessary edification, that it may impart grace to the hearers."

This strategy of the enemy was sent to ground you and lower your self-esteem! You must be able to handle or respond to criticism well. You cannot escape this attack! Everyone in Christ will be confronted by some form of criticism. It is a vehicle that God allows the enemy to use as a tool to mature us. You cannot bypass it. It will always be knocking at your door to test your response—good, bad, or ugly. Choose to allow this tool of the enemy to shape your character and capacity.

As one who is being used by God, you must know how to limit the amount of criticism around you. Do not let this strategy of the enemy turn your response into a personal attack against others who are positively standing with you.

With the right attitude and godly wisdom, you will be able to overcome the combined forces exposed in this chapter.

Chapter 11

THE POSITIONING OF THE SONS OF GOD, PAST, PRESENT, AND FUTURE

I N EACH GENERATION, God will always have a designated group who will stay true to Him and His will as it is made known to them. They will not yield to the temptation of man's influence. They will take up their position and exercise spiritual authority that is needed in the Kingdom to influence and affect the outcome of the warfare that each generation will endure, leading to ever-increasing victory. They will not compromise.

God has placed into their hands the ability to unlock the divine strategies of heaven and enforce them on this earth. They are a different breed of leadership that has been equipped by God to oversee the advancement of the Kingdom here on earth for the next phase of growth in the Body. They are pioneers in this realm and have grown to the level of maturity that is needed in this season in the Body. They know how to get the job done and are strong in their commitment to God and His ways. They are aggressive and violent in their faith and could be perceived as arrogant.

Some of the skilled warriors and mature saints are now passing away. If they were good stewards of their mantles, then we will have another generation trained to enforce the decrees of the Kingdom of heaven on the earth and push forward the agenda of God.

If they did not—God forbid!—many in the Body will have to go through a phase where they will be forced to confront intense opposition so that those who are unskilled and lack spiritual authority in the ways of God can get the necessary experience. There will be casualties.

> *Now these are the nations which the LORD left, that He might test Israel by them, that is, all who had not known any of the wars in Canaan (this was only so that the generations of the children of Israel might be taught to know war, at least those who had not formerly known it).*
>
> — Judges 3:1-2

According to a report by Linda Robinson in the *US News and World Report*, "A Few More Good Men":

> *The US armed forces changed the way they train and deploy the different branches of their armed forces. The rules of engagement have changed in the countries that they are at war with and the*

strategies of the enemies have at times brought challenges that they have never encountered before. In order to push back the enemies and maintain an advantage, the armed forces are increasing their special forces, including the way they are trained. They must have a percentage of veterans re-enlist in order for the success of the program. Along with trying to fill the ranks, the concern is about stanching the loss of experienced operators who are the backbone of the small teams that work unsupervised in distant lands. The success of the entire venture ultimately depends on whether the military's overall re-enlistment rate holds up. Two slogans were adopted as reminders of this painful lesson of past wars: **Quality is more important than quantity, and special operators cannot be mass-produced.**

Seasoning. *Many technological innovations help turn out more elite units faster. But it is inevitable that expansion, in the short run, will produce a force that is younger and less experienced in special ops. Time will season them, assuming they re-enlist. Experience and maturity are particularly vital to Special Forces and other units that operate without higher commands nearby. Their structure reflects the degree* *of responsibility entrusted to them. (Emphasis added)*

The sons of God in this hour must take up their positions so that the Kingdom can increase to the measure that God has designated.

> *For as many as are led by the Spirit of God, these are sons of God.... For the earnest expectation of the creation eagerly waits for the revealing of the sons of God.*
>
> — Romans 8:14, 19

They do not seek out others in the religious/political arena in the Body for affirmation of their calling. They choose to wait on God and His providence to manifest and make a way for them to fulfill His delight. They waste very little time in finding those to whom they can impart the mantles, wisdom, and experience that they have gained in Christ to ensure that the next generation will have a remnant who will remain faithful to God.

They are swift to put to death the areas in their lives that can bring them to a screeching halt. They wear victories like a tapestry of scars in their spirits, which have been forged from intense warfare. It is a testimony to God's grace and unending commitment in building His Kingdom in and through earthen vessels co-laboring for the fullness of His divine will in each phase.

Chapter 12

CHANGING THE STATUS QUO: THE GAME CHANGERS

THERE ARE THOSE who have been called to navigate skillfully when seasons demand decisive actions that will steer the course of organizations, businesses, cities, nations, families, and individuals when they reach a turning point. These individuals are sought after because of their particular skill sets that are needed to stabilize and reposition organizations for strategic growth and prosperity. They are known as the game changers who have the abilities and capacity to steer organizations in a particular direction. These individuals can bear up under the weight of circumstances and the critical phase that is confronting them. They were employed for such a critical phase in the growth and development of an organization.

So it is in the spiritual world. The game changers will go against all traditions and defy the mentality of "this is the way we have always done it." Those who cannot forget yesterday's achievements and success—those who spend their precious time in reminiscing about past victories—will never be able to receive the download of fresh revelations or instructions to stay on course and fulfill their assignments. You must strategically position yourself and focus on the Kingdom business at hand.

That is where you, the burden bearers, come in, the ones who have been given the task to take authority over and against the forces of darkness and bring to a screeching halt the plans of the enemy. You are the ones who God has selected to become game changers. The task at hand may seem insurmountable, but God called you who have accepted the assignment. God knows all about the challenges and times of hardship and difficulties you will encounter along the way. He knows your pain, discouragement, and the oppressive situations that the enemy will use to try to keep you as a prisoner. God will never give you an assignment and not prepare you for it.

> *God will never give you an assignment and not prepare you for it.*

You may have the passion and zeal, but without the seasons of preparation, you will falter or start tripping up through entanglements and pitfalls that the enemy will throw at you. Hard work is a character trait of a warrior. Without the seasons of preparation, you will not make it. Skillful warriors will always be found working hard. Praying is the hard work you must do.

Many go from church to church and do not develop strong, deep roots. Stop jumping from place to place and wait for God to shift you. If you believe that you know more than God, you will end up bypassing the seasons of preparation and miss vital steps in your assignment. I pray that you will fulfill the ministry that God gave you and not be like the servant Jesus warned us about in the parable of the talents. You will be judged base on the level of fulfilling your calling.

> *And cast the unprofitable servant into the outer darkness. There will be weeping and gnashing of teeth.*
>
> — Matthew 25:30

The true intercessors must stand their ground and not waver. They are frequently in the presence of God in deep intercession, groaning and wrestling with principalities, strongmen, wicked human agents, and all types of beasts in the spirit realm in order for others to move ahead and become successful in their assignments.

Let us look at two individuals, their responses, and the impact of them receiving their assignments. Paul and Ananias were both game changers. God revealed Himself and gave instructions to both at turning points in their lives that were pivotal for His plan of redemption.

Paul was formerly known as Saul, and was persecuting the Church!

This I also did in Jerusalem, and many of the saints I shut up in prison, having received authority from the chief priests; and when they were put to death, I cast my vote against them. And I punished them often in every synagogue and compelled them to blaspheme; and being exceedingly enraged against them, I persecuted them even to foreign cities.

— Acts 26:10-11

Saul did not hesitate or question our Lord Jesus when He revealed Himself to him on the road to Damascus. God, in His sovereign will, selected him for His redemptive purposes—yes, the one who was persecuting the Church.

As he traveled he approached Damascus, and suddenly a light from heaven flashed around him [displaying the glory and majesty of Christ]; and he fell to the ground and heard a voice [from heaven] saying to him, "Saul, Saul, why are you persecuting and oppressing Me?" And Saul said, "Who are You, Lord?" And He answered, "I am Jesus whom you are persecuting, now get up and go into the city, and you will be told what you must do."

— Acts 9:3-6 AMP

God had a plan to rescue and use Paul to bring the Gentiles into the plan of redemption. Paul responded by submitting to the call and accepting the assignment. He recognized Jesus as his Lord and Savior and dedicated his life to obeying Him.

> *Get up and stand on your feet. I have appeared to you for this purpose, to appoint you [to serve] as a minister and as a witness [to testify, with authority,] not only to the things which you have seen, but also to the things in which I will appear to you, [choosing you for Myself and] rescuing you from the Jewish people and from the Gentiles, to whom I am sending you, to open their [spiritual] eyes so that they may turn from darkness to light and from the power of Satan to God, that they may receive forgiveness and release from their sins and an inheritance among those who have been sanctified (set apart, made holy) by faith in Me.*
>
> — Acts 26:16-18 AMP

Paul was given the assignment and accepted it without having to get a confirmation from another person. There are times that we need to seek counsel or get confirmation, so do not use this as a template for following every instruction you receive from God. The Bible references using wise advice as we move forward: "Where there is no counsel, the people fall; But in the multitude of counselors there is safety" (Prov. 11:14).

Ananias was called by God and given instruction to go and minister to Paul, but like many of us will, he gave excuses and doubted God's plan for others, due to what he heard about them. God had to assure Ananias that He had chosen Paul for a specific assignment. He finally submitted to God and ministered to Paul.

> *But the Lord said to him, "Go, for this man is a [deliberately] chosen instrument of Mine, to bear My name before the Gentiles and kings and the sons of Israel; for I will make clear to him how much he must suffer and endure for My name's sake." So Ananias left and entered the house, and he laid his hands on Saul and said, "Brother Saul, the Lord Jesus, who appeared to you on the road as you came [to Damascus], has sent me so that you may regain your sight and be filled with the Holy Spirit [in order to proclaim Christ to both Jews and Gentiles]."*
> — Acts 9:15-17 AMP

The Bible records that Paul mentioned Ananias in Acts 22, but no other information is given about Ananias. What type of relationship did they have after their initial meeting that was orchestrated by God? Can you overcome fear and the misgivings concerning God's chosen vessels in spite of what you have witnessed or heard about them prior to the call of God upon their lives?

They both responded slightly differently to the call and the instructions they were given. Do you have an assignment like Paul? Or like Ananias? What has been your response? You were called specifically to change the status quo and shift the Kingdom agenda against contrary winds and storms. That is the responsibility of the game changers.

Let us look at another example. In Matthew 15:22-28, there was a woman from the borders of Canaan who came to where Jesus was and kept crying out for Him to deliver her daughter who was demon-possessed. He did not respond to her request, and His disciples told Him to make her go away because she was troubling them with her constant cry for help. He then said to her that He was sent to bring the miraculous power of God only to the Jews and therefore could not give it to someone who did not meet the requirements or qualifications. She stood her ground and refused to be turned away. She did not allow their opposition to deter from her assignment—getting her daughter healed. She showed great faith—believing that the miraculous power of God was the only solution for her daughter's situation.

> *And behold, a woman of Canaan came from that region and cried out to Him, saying, "Have mercy on me, O Lord, Son of David! My daughter is severely demon-possessed." But He answered her not a word. And His disciples*

*came and urged Him, saying, "Send her away,
for she cries out after us." But He answered and
said, "I was not sent except to the lost sheep of
the house of Israel." Then she came and wor-
shiped Him, saying, "Lord, help me!" But He
answered and said, "It is not good to take the
children's bread and throw it to the little dogs."
And she said, "Yes, Lord, yet even the little dogs
eat the crumbs which fall from their masters'
table." Then Jesus answered and said to her, "O
woman, great is your faith! Let it be to you as
you desire." And her daughter was healed from
that very hour.*

This woman refused to accept that she did not meet the
qualifications for a recipient of a miracle. She was compelled by the love she had for her daughter and nobody
would hinder her, not even the one God was using. The
rules of engagement for a miracle changed in her favor by
the level of confidence she had in the power of God.

Game changers must be bold, courageous, full of faith,
humble, and walk in the power of the Holy Ghost. This
example below will push you to an outrageous and bold
faith in God's abilities.

*Then came the daughters of Zelophehad the son
of Hepher, the son of Gilead, the son of Machir,
the son of Manasseh, from the families of*

*Manasseh the son of Joseph; and these were the
names of his daughters: Mahlah, Noah, Hoglah,
Milcah, and Tirzah.*

— Numbers 27:1

It is recorded in the Bible in the Book of Numbers that
there were five daughters of a man named Zelophehad
who would not be able to hold onto their father's inheritance because they were not sons. They had a cause and
became game changers!

*"Why should the name of our father be removed
from among his family because he had no
son? Give us a possession among our father's
brothers." So Moses brought their case before the
LORD. And the LORD spoke to Moses, saying:
"The daughters of Zelophehad speak what is
right; you shall surely give them a possession of
inheritance among their father's brothers, and
cause the inheritance of their father to pass to
them."*

— Numbers 27:4-7

When Moses was taking a census in preparation for
dividing the Promised Land as God had instructed, the
daughters of Zelophehad went to him with sheer deter-
mination, much humility, courage, and great faith in
God and His character, and demanded justice. The laws
in those times stated that only men inherited land and

property, and women were listed as property. Their request was very well-presented and required much deliberation. Moses had to bring the matter before God, who responded that Zelophehad's daughters were correct to state that the laws were unjust because of their situation. Why should their father's inheritance be given to someone else because there were no sons born in that family? God told Moses to change the laws to include women moving forward.

Can God count on you to be the one who will go against the grain and stand up for an outcome that everyone is saying "cannot be done" even if they present a strong case why your assignment will not be successful and can prove that the law is against your cause?

Chapter 13

A NEW TIME AND SEASON

YOU ARE A target for the onslaught of the enemy. He will stir up troubling situations against you to hold you down in the pits of despair and depression, but you will rise up from the pits and the ashes of discouragement and oppression to take up your cause and run with it.

> *Shake yourself from the dust, arise; Sit down,*
> *O Jerusalem! Loose yourself from the bonds of*
> *your neck, O captive daughter of Zion!*
> — Isaiah 52:2

God cannot afford to allow the enemy to take you out prematurely, before you complete your divine assignment. The intercessors are being stirred up in the nations to place fiery fervent prayers on their altars to bring the Hand of God onto the scene so that the chains that have held you down can be broken so you can start or continue in your assignment.

The overwhelming bombardments from the satanic and witchcraft kingdom will frustrate your assignment by depleting your spiritual strength, but one of the methods that God uses to help us is the prophetic ministry that can remove this frustration by revealing the plan of God, giving you a jump start, and unlocking the new time and season in your life. The accuracy of the prophetic word released can set you on the correct path for your destiny to be fulfilled. We need true and accurate prophets more than ever! The new time and season are knocking at your door, demanding the maturing of your gifts and character. Many are depending on you!

When prophets issue challenges, they tend to bring disruptions in your structured environment. You then have to make a decision whether or not to change direction, make the necessary changes, follow the new instructions, or stay committed to what you have been familiar with. Staying in your comfort zone can abort or derail your destiny and put you in a place of stagnation and non-accomplishment.

The Gospel of Jesus Christ brings confrontation in any environment! It demands change and must be preached without apology to convert and bring changes to the different environments around us. You have to be willing to move as the Spirit of God moves. You will be required to always make a decision! There will always be a response to the Gospel—to yield or not to yield; adapt, adjust, move, or take a wait-and-see attitude. It is God's search-and-rescue operation, and He needs you!

"Obedient to the cause" is your commitment. Your assignment demands a relevant response. You cannot be indecisive and hesitant.

You will be anointed to run as Elijah ran and overtook Ahab's chariot. He had the endurance and speed to run about fourteen miles and stay ahead of the King's chariot. That was the supernatural Hand of God upon him. Let the zeal of the Lord come upon you in your willingness to serve and demonstrate the power of God. You will overtake many who have gone on before you in their assignments.

> *"Obedient to the cause" is your commitment.*

> *Then the hand of the LORD came upon Elijah; and he girded up his loins and ran ahead of Ahab to the entrance of Jezreel.*
>
> — 1 Kings 18:46

All setbacks are a setup for God's glory to come on the scene. God is with you and will deliver, keep, protect, and meet all your needs. He will never bring dishonor and shame upon you.

Burden bearers, we must cry out continually for those in our generation to make it as well as those who God has predestined down through the generations. There is no failure in God and He does not make mistakes. You have been handpicked for such a time as this. Burden bearers, let the fire—your intercession—be continually upon the altar as you stay faithful in fulfilling your God-given assignments.

God has not lost any of His creation; He has never misplaced or forgotten where He has put something. All creation are kept and sustained by Him. He has placed a higher value and honor on mankind over all His creation. He would destroy man-made systems, shake the heavens, level mountains, change the heart of man towards you and your assignment, and release the host of heaven to watch over all that concerns you. God cannot fail!

> *Therefore, my beloved brethren, be steadfast, immovable, always abounding in the work of the Lord, knowing that your labor is not in vain in the Lord.*
>
> — 1 Corinthians 15:58

I declare your ministry will be resilient, relevant, and trans-generational.

I command all obstacles to be taken out of your way as you gain the strength to move forward. I command all your adversaries to be taken into captivity and the yoke of afflictions to be destroyed. I declare total restoration of your physical body, your ministry, and your finances. Let there be divine provisions, connections, and opportunities for your assignment.

"Therefore all those who devour you shall be devoured; And all your adversaries, every one of them, shall go into captivity; Those who plunder you shall become plunder, And all who prey upon you I will make a prey. For I will restore health to you And heal you of your wounds," says the LORD, "Because they called you an outcast saying: 'This is Zion; No one seeks her.'"
— Jeremiah 30:16-17

Chapter 14

THE PROCESSING: A POINT OF NO RETURN

OD KNOWS THE process that is necessary in order for the manifestation of His sons to fulfill their assignments. Turing back is not an option for them. They are persuaded that in every season, no matter the circumstances, they will give birth to their seed of destiny.

When one is about to give birth to the seed of destiny, discomfort sets in through fatigue, sickness, financial challenges, seed killers, obstacles, and trials. One must be equipped to overcome these challenges.

These sons are sensitive to the Holy Spirit and know the cost of obedience. They also know that God never aborts His plan or abandons His children. These seasons of birthing are where they fight and travail in order to usher in the glory of God in and through their lives.

They have learned that those who encourage them in the beginning stage are now unable to do so and have gone as far as they were anointed to go. They are also very cautious of those who they allow in the delivery room—the final stage that will position them for increase.

They appreciate those who have helped to nurture them along the way, but understand that they may not be qualified to help in the delivery process and are not moved by their emotional trials. They will not be held hostage by the prison of "obligation" and "manipulation," but will be willing servants to the will of God.

The travailing process is necessary and cannot be skipped in pursuit of the promises of God. We must give birth only to what remains after the shaking or stripping away in this stage of the process. It is the place where we are presented with the opportunity to increase in our ability to endure—to suffer.

It is also the stage in which opposition intensifies to bring visible the dross, the areas in our character that God has targeted to be dealt with. The old revelations and anointing are purged. It is also where:

- Our reasonings are dealt with
- Any residue of doubt is removed
- We let go of anything that will weigh one down
- The cover of deception is removed
- We draw closer to God
- We enter into a deeper level of sensitivity to the Holy Spirit
- We have increased hunger for the presence of God
- We ascend to the heights and depths of faith in God

These sons have learned to identify and halt prideful thoughts that will lure them into believing that what they carry is greater than what others are carrying.

This travailing stage is the time where, glancing over their shoulders, they can see that they have gone beyond the halfway mark of this process, and it is not beneficial to stay where they are. The bridge that took them over

Going back is not an option.

has now collapsed, and the door behind them is closed. Going back is not an option.

At times, the sheer agony of this season is immeasurable. This is the place where they see the value and worth of the treasure that they are carrying and the impact that will ripple down through the generations that are yet to be born in Christ.

They now have positioned themselves for an outpouring of the grace of God as they birth character, gifts, ministries, relationships, careers, and businesses. They are simultaneously being stretched and strengthened for the advancement of God's Kingdom. Here is where they passed the point of no return.

No one can fulfill their call until they give up everything. You must endeavor to finish your assignment and allow God to establish His counsel through you.

Chapter 15

ESTABLISHING THE WORKS OF GOD

Believe in the LORD your God, and you shall be established; believe His prophets, and you shall prosper.

— 2 Chronicles 20:20

FAITH IN GOD's divine abilities is why this breed of the sons of God is released in this phase of the redemptive plan of God. It is God who has chosen them to establish His work.

He knows what you have become at the stage of perfection before you accepted the assignment. God will use your highs and lows, disappointments, attacks, suffering, and difficulties to forge His character in you as He equips you!

I love this description that God gave to me in times of intercession so I can declare over your lives who you are in Christ and the traits that must be established in you. He said to me, "*Their movements are swift and decisive as the Holy Ghost releases upon them the boldness and courage that is needed to endure the necessary warfare. They are able to see the enemy afar off and with precision put in place the divine strategies for securing, maintaining, and advancing the Kingdom of God. They are not easily manipulated by the seduction and craftiness of temptations and witchcraft. They will be resilient, able to endure, and committed to the task at hand."*

These sons of God in this hour are committed to God's plan in every phase. They must bring the Body out from under the influence of the enemy's snares and back under the authority of God through righteousness by faith. The authority has been given to them to bring about the shifting of power into the hands of the people of God.

> *These sons of God in this hour are committed to God's plan in every phase.*

The mark of grace is upon them and they wear the zeal of the Lord like a cloak to advance the Kingdom. They diligently seek out those who will stay true to His purposes, yielding continually to the Holy Spirit to bring them to a place of maturity in character and gifts to ensure that the integrity of the teachings and application of Christ is established in every phase of growth in their generation.

When we increase in understanding, we can receive clarity and are able to take the relevant course of action. The prophetic instructions that are birthed out of revelation from God are invaluable and can thrust one into destiny and greatness.

A decree has been released by the Spirit of the Lord that the sons of God must manifest in this hour. They are valiant, strong, aggressive, and full of faith and of the power of the Holy Ghost. They are those who have the courage, boldness, and skills necessary to establish victories for the Kingdom and its advancement in this phase of warfare.

I declare, let the burden bearers—the intercessors—be mantled, strengthened, and encouraged for the grace of God to be poured out upon them as they labor with the Holy Ghost to legislate in detailing out in intercession the plans and purposes of God for His sons. These game changers will fulfill their God-given assignments in their generation and for those who have yet to be born.

IF YOU ENJOYED THIS BOOK, WILL YOU HELP ME SPREAD THE WORD?

There are several ways you can help me get the word out about the message of this book...

- Post a 5-Star review on Amazon.

- Write about the book on your Facebook, Twitter, Instagram, LinkedIn – any social media you regularly use!

- If you blog, consider referencing the book, or publishing an excerpt from the book with a link back to my website. You have my permission to do this as long as you provide proper credit and backlinks.

- Recommend the book to friends – word-of-mouth is still the most effective form of advertising.

- Purchase additional copies to give away as gifts.

The best way to connect is by visiting
www.rachelcarter.org